*Lethal Frequencies*

# Lethal Frequencies

James Galvin

*J. Gal.*

*Chicago (snow) '98*

COPPER CANYON PRESS

Publication of this book is supported by a grant from the National Endowment
for the Arts and a grant from the Lannan Foundation. Additional support to
Copper Canyon Press has been provided by the Andrew W. Mellon Foundation,
the Lila Wallace–Reader's Digest Fund, and the Washington State Arts
Commission. Copper Canyon Press is in residence with Centrum at Fort Worden
State Park.

*Library of Congress Cataloging-in-Publication Data*
Galvin, James.
Lethal Frequencies : poems / by James Galvin.
p. cm.
ISBN 1-55659-069-5
I. Title.
PS3557.A444L48 1994
811'.54 – DC20
94-31305

COPPER CANYON PRESS
P.O. BOX 271, PORT TOWNSEND, WASHINGTON 98368

# Acknowledgments

The magazines some of these poems appeared in are:

*Ars Poetica*
*The Antioch Review*
*The Atlantic*
*Boulevard*
*Coe Review*
*The Colorado Review*
*Cut Bank*
*Field*
*The Iowa Review*
*The New Yorker*
*Paris Review*
*Quarterly West*

"Small Countries" is page 131 from *The Meadow*, by James Galvin, Henry Holt, 1992.

# Contents

*Lethal Frequencies*

# Hell to Breakfast

*for Steve Adkisson*

Stevie, vandals smashed
The fretless you made me I
Hear it

# Independence Day, 1956, A Fairy Tale

I think this house's mouth is full of dirt.
                    Smoke is nothing up its sleeve.
I think it could explode.
              Where I am, in the dirt under the floor, I hear
them.
      They don't know.
             My mother leaves each room my father enters.
                                        Now
she is cleaning things that are already clean.
                        My father is in the living
room.
      He's pouring.
              Rum into a glass, gas into a lamp, kerosene into a can.
He pours capped fuses, matches, dynamite sticks into his pockets.
                                  He pours
rounds into the .45 which he will point skyward and hold next to his ear
as if it were telling him things.
                      Where I am, the spider spins.
                              The broken
mouse drags a trap through lunar talc of dust.
                            Where the bitch whelps is
where I wriggle on my belly, cowardly, ashamed, to escape the Fourth of
July.
      I think the house is very ready.
                      It seems to hover like an "exploded
view" in a repair manual.
                  Parts suspended in disbelief.
                            Nails pulled back,
aimed.
      My father goes out.
              My mother whimpers.
                      There'll be no supper.
She opens the firebox and stuffs it full of forks.

# The Weather Spider

### 1.

A spider lives in the barometer.
It's a white spider and it was born there.

Sometimes it rains from a clear blue sky.
Or rain falls without touching the ground.

Or it doesn't rain.
Of course we had weather before the spider,

Before the barometer, so it isn't that.
We have thunder in winter, dry lightning

Unravelling the tree and the three good horses under it,
Snow leaving the earth and

Falling straight up, back into the cloud.
Anybody got a match?

Anybody got a thimbleful of blood?

### 2.

After a slim night storm
The spidery likenesses of aspens
Memorize the north sides

Of the trees themselves.
Wouldn't it be wrong to say
The new buds *wait*, sheathed in ice?

Do you think the spider doesn't *matter* to weather
Just because it lives in the barometer?
The first light seems to like it

In these glass branches.
The whole morning is given
To unilateral disarmament

Of all sides.
Beneath the glass
The spider's indifference towards us

Grows immense, indomitable.
Anybody got a thimbleful of blood?

# Art Class

Let us begin with a simple line,
Drawn as a child would draw it,
to indicate the horizon,

More real than the real horizon,
Which is less than line,
Which is visible abstraction, a ratio.

The line ravishes the page with implications
Of white earth, white sky!

The horizon moves as we move,
Making us feel central.
But the horizon is an empty shell —

Strange radius whose center is peripheral.
As the horizon draws us on, withdrawing,
The line draws us in,

Requiring further lines,
Engendering curves, verticals, diagonals,
Urging shades, shapes, figures....

What should we place, in all good faith,
On the horizon? A stone?
An empty chair? A submarine?

Take your time. Take it easy.
The horizon will not stop abstracting us.

# On Exploration

A hawk drops to the treetop
Like a falling cross.
The haybarn is ticking.
The Universe has everything.
That's what I like about it.
A single chubby cloud
Bee-lines downwind
Trying to catch up with the others.

Yellow leaves plane across the water,
Drifting the inlet.
The pond is a droozy eye.
Details tend to equal each other,
Making decisions harder.
Is polio an endangered species?
The Universe is mostly empty,
That's important;
A fractal palindrome of concentric

Emptinesses.
Is there life out there?
Are there lawns?
Columbus is famous for discovering a place
Where there were already people
Killing each other.
Nothing missing. Nothing new.

Let's pick wildflowers.
Let's take a meteor shower.
Let's live forever and let's die, too.

# Two Horses and a Dog

Without external reference,
The world presents itself
In perfect clarity.

Wherewithal, arrested moments,
The throes of demystification,
Morality as nothing more
Than humility and honesty, a salty measure.

Then it was a cold snap,
Weather turned lethal so it was easier
To feel affinity
With lodgepole stands, rifted aspens,
And grim, tenacious sage.

History accelerates till it misses the turns.
Wars are shorter now
Just to fit into it.

One day you know you are no longer young
Because you've stopped loving your own desperation.
You change *life* to *loneliness* in your mind
And, you know, you need to change it back.

Statistics show that
One in every five
Women
Is essential to my survival.

My daughter asks how wide is lightning.
That depends, but I don't know on what.
Probably the dimension of inner hugeness,
As in a speck of dirt.

It was an honor to suffer humiliation and refusal.
Shame was an honor.
It was an honor to freeze your ass horseback
In the year's first blizzard,
Looking for strays that never materialized.

It was an honor to break apart against this,
An honor to fail at well-being
As the high peaks accepted the first snow –
A sigh of relief.

Time stands still
And we and things so whizzing past it,
Queasy and lonely,
Wearing dogtags with scripture on them.

## Listen Hard

Enough and you can hear
The small breakages occurring.
That's what all sounds are:
Small sounds, small things breaking;
Big sounds, big things breaking.

Think of a drop of water
Flung from the grindstone.
It's always day, it's always night.
No such thing as tomorrow.

There's a match going out.
There's paying for privilege.
There's harm's way,

It's all the same day.
Sunlight drools on the grass.
An air of faded intimacy.

Listen to the sound of the pages turning.
Listen to the sound of the book when it closes.

# A Portrait of My Roof

My steel roof mirrors clouds
Like a book the sky left off reading.

The story of clouds passing keeps passing,
As stories will, even with the book turned over,

Even closed, shelved, forgotten;
Inside I leave off working

And turn my notebook spine up to wonder
What kind of story is boring the sky.

I don't have to go far for the answer.
I don't have to go anywhere.

Shall I take up serpents for interest?
I have taken up serpents.

Shall I refuse happiness?
For interest?

No, I shall claim the obvious,
That hearts are no exclusive province.

I shall go outside and lie down in the grass.
I shall read the passing clouds,

Chaotic, senseless, wise,
Unlike anything one finds in reflection.

# More Like It

### 1.

It's white ashes
That drift and mizzle,
Muffle and sift like snow.

Feather-ash, not snow.
Sure sign Heaven
Has burned to the ground again.

The pines
(Ah, Unanimous!)
Elect a new God.

### 2.

The jetstream careens
As if with a new God at the wheel.

The pines never stop praying.
They pray best in a drizzle.

The pines pray up a drought.
They pray snowdrifts and sheet lightning.

They get everything they pray for.
They get sex with the wind.

### 3.

Pine pollen yellows the air
Thick as smoke.
Woodgrain flames inside the pines,
Insatiable, flames
Like palms pressed together.

4.
Here in pines under ashen sky
I am. Reason is
To join my prayers
With theirs.

# The War That Isn't What You Think

The little wind I saw curving and lifting
The black mare's mane
Never came this way,
Though I waited, face tilted:
To wind as heliotropic is to sun.

We have to keep our disappointment alive.
We have to sustain our appal, act surprised
That humanity has (again today!)
Failed to evolve away from meanness.
That we ourselves have failed in this.

Invisible earth,
I still can't feel any wind,
Can't feel though I hear cottonwood leaves that hung still
Turn sudden, turn all-at-once,
Like small birds in a flight of small birds, turning,

Like one thing instead of many,
Turn silver side to the wind when it comes,
Shiver and moan when it comes.
O wind, immaculate, that lifts the mane,
Immaculate, that turns the silver leaves,
That bears away the smoke of sacrifice.

The wind, when it finds me, bears no trace
Of sage-sweet horsesmell, no color black,
No softness of muzzle of the
Mare, her mane curving and lifting,
Where she grazes the horizon down to nothing.

## One Day

For all intents and purposes
The President is folded away for the night.

It's been a bad day
For intents and purposes.

After all is said and done
No one should have said anything.

We should have done otherwise.
It was a terrible day for saying and doing.

People with spectacles were asked to stand forward.
Owls went up in smoke.

What could anyone do about evil or suffering
On a day like this.

Dogs howled in pain from a lethal frequency.
Lovers fell silent and drifted into separate distances.

It was a day, oh – everywhere you turned
A molten angel stood in the way.

# I Looked for Life
## and Did a Shadow See

Some little splinter
Of shadow purls
And weals down
The slewed stone
Chapel steps,
Slinks along
The riverrock wall
And disappears
Into the light.
Now ropy, riffled,
Now owlish, sere,
It smolders back
To sight beneath
A dwarfish, brindled tree
That chimes and sifts
And resurrects
In something's sweet
And lethal breath.
This little shadow
Seems to know
(How can it know?
How can it not?)
Just when to flinch
Just where to loop and sag
And skitter down,
Just what to squirrel
And what to squander till
The light it lacks
Bleeds it back
And finds
My sleeping dark-haired girl –
O personal,

Impersonal,
Continual thrall –
And hammocks blue
In the hollows of her eyes.

# Indirective

The ridge road takes the ridgespine every way
It turns. It threads the granite vertibrae
And old, wind-dwarfed ponderosas that twist
Out of the ungiving, unforgiving ground
Like tips of auger bits drilled through from Hell.
Here, all trees die by lightning soon or late.
This hidden side-trail elk hunters found will fall
To their camp on Sheep Creek, where the creek stops them.
They ignite their Colemans, dress the carcasses,
Make drunk display in artificial light.
Years past the road kept going, forded there.
Now the creek has cut and caved the bank.
You have to go on horseback or afoot.
Well, just as well. Afoot or horseback was
The only way to go before the road,
Before the reason for the road arrived,
Disguised as some old trapper, moonshiner,
Xenophobe, or who the hell he was –
Old badger, anyway, who cleared some trees,
Cut some sidehill and creekbank with a slip
And mule to get a wagon way in there
With stores to keep him winterlong and when
The water rose too high to ford, Lord knows.
I said I'd take you there but I don't know.
More than likely I'll just get us lost.
The last time I tried to find the old homestead
I poked around for it awhile and then
Rode on to look for some of Richard's strays.
I never saw a cow that day either.
But I'll take you up and we can look
If your heart's set on it. The only time
I saw the place myself I was with Ray.
Well, now Ray's dead, but he knew where it was.
Back then you could still drive there four-wheel-drive,

Before the crossing disappeared. Even
Then the bank was steep for Ray's old Scout.
We lost the clutch, but Ray still got us there.
The nearby spring doesn't give it away,
Popping out like it does from solid
Rock, where even willows will not grow,
And diving underground before you know it,
As if it didn't like it here above.
What it looks like, in case we come up empty,
It looks small, just part of the woods, but small,
The cabin I mean, its logs obscured by brush.
It's dwarfed by the size of trunks surrounding it.
Deep snow country grows big trees. They vault
And loom in shadowed unconcern. The cabin
Is squalid, yes, but mostly it looks dim,
Or maybe brief would be the way to say it –
Depressing brevity we recognize
As squalor. Not much sun in woods like those,
None inside the windowless log shack.
Let's touch our horses up across this park.
That grove yonder might just be the one.
That time I came up here with Ray, God rest,
The time we found the place – it's only six
Or seven logs in height and ten feet square –
The door was ajar and stingy with its dark.
I noticed that before I saw the roof
Caved in, which made that depth of dark seem strange.
It kind of chilled me when we found the spine
Of something human-sized right by the door.
Ray mentioned, *There's no need to close the door
Behind you if you're going out to die.*
It was half-buried. I'm not saying it
*Was* a man, just that it could have been.
I wouldn't know a spine of bear from man
Or woman, would you? I'll be damned. We're here.
It all looks just the same. The spine is gone.
What's that? A skull, sure as hell, half-buried,

Or half-unburied, like a blind white eye
In the ground. Relax. It isn't human.
More like an old badger. See the teeth? Here
The only human bones are yours and mine.

## *Sapphic Suicide Note*

day out
no worldly joy
italics mine

## Speaking Terms

All around me to-ing and fro-ing
In a strapping south wind
Pine boughs lisp their approval
Of moving without moving around, saying,
Shh! This way! Shh! This way!
They contradict each other
By all saying the same thing.

Better to impersonate than to
Personify, when it comes to nature.
Shh! I tell them, This way!
And start walking.

# Trespassers

Now, on this new page,
A new optimism groans into place.
The leaves, like extras
One is beginning to know by name,
Sigh and lift perceptibly.
A doe steps into the clearing and looks toward the house –
Just checking – then turns and highsteps
With exaggerated precision, flight held in,
Back to cover.
Two hunters,
Trespassing but willing to claim
They are lost, mistaken, sorry,
Simmer in the throaty idle of their pickup,
Gazing down into a deep draw.
They pull away slowly. They'll be back.
The day itself is good.
Whatever happens in the day,
The day itself is good.
A breeze tensely riffles the pond,
Erasing the pond's attempt at representation
Of treetops and sky – try again.
It keeps doing that.
A jet goes over and you rise to build a fire.
As if the jet were a signal.
One hunter says good day, though,
Even if we don't get anything.
Nice weather.
And the deer step out of the woods
As if drawn by a magnet.

# Right Now

The Mind assumes The Position
Under a cocaine moon.
Flip.
Live it up.
De-tox, re-tox, just like tides.
Shouldn'a, wouldn'a.
Ifn't.
There is no shadow without a field
To fall on.
Tomorrow we can say, "Tomorrow".
Don't tell me the truth will set you free.
It's too busy making you a hero.
As for critics, they don't know.
They'll never know. They're not supposed to know.
Acedia aside,
Acceptance is the only way that grace survives.
In us.
Us shadows with no field to fall on.
The violins were slobbering.
There were heavy buildings
There were plenty of anxious people, crying,
"That men may not forget me utterly."
So there was a bonfire made of oars.
There was.
Without you I'd be heartless.
I'd say, "Be there when it all goes wrong!"
I might be stupid but I ain't slow.
I don't believe in a world
You could lose in a heartbeat.

## Resurrection Update

And then it happened.
Amidst cosmic busting and booming
Gravity snapped,
That galactic rack and pinion.

Trees took off like rockets.
Cemeteries exploded.
The living and the dead
Flew straight up together.

Only up was gone. Up was away.
Earth still spun
As it stalled and drifted darkward,
Sublime,

An aspirin in a glass of water.

# Untitled, 1968

*for Mark Rothko*

There's no such thing as an emergency.

Betrayal is eventual.

The bridge is a river, when you think about it.

River of blood,

when you think about it.

The Lord giveth.

Highest echelons of

quietude.

A veronica in each sunset.

In every blackening bandage

in the hospital's unspeakable bins, a veronica.

Someone suffered

here.

The elevator full of blood rose like any other.

Why not.

Our nets were full of sunset when we hauled them in.

The red sail

filled and pulled us darkward.

Blood in the drumroll blossomed.

The Lord giveth.

Thou shalt.

Change the bandages when they blacken.

Don't think about it.

Set the red sail and disappear.

Slow drip

in silence.

Don't say a word.

Don't say the wineglass on the sill

is a sun-dried sangreal.

It's a landscape.

You just can't bring

your body.

The bridge is an inward horizon.
The bridge has arrived
in time for us to cross.
I know because someone, or his assistant,
suffered here.

# You Know What People Say

Sulky what-ifs.
Sulky what-ifs.
They bumblefuck the metastuff.
Diffidence their stock in trade.
Cozy hell – cozy, hell.
They make a mockery of irony.
They hold Special Olympics in wit.
What was Shakespeare's blood pressure?
Vertical river, cloister of thunder,
Bleeds the ship's fell sail.
God comes in for a landing. He lowers God's landing gear.
He raises the holy spoilers, lowers the sacred ailerons. He imagines
Reality.
Tried everything in life?
Sulky what-ifs are dumbstruck. Drumsticks
Their spiritual actuality is empirical.
What if uppity angels?
What if there really were rules?
What if those angels melted in the rain?
If reality is illusion, wouldn't it stand to reason
That illusions are real?
A lot of dumb questions.
Impingement of external objects or conditions upon the body
Palpitate apostasy.
The oppressed must free the oppressors to free themselves, see?
The soul is euphemism for the body.
What does *willing* mean? Do you sense my sense?
Am I fashionable?
Objective as an angel in the rain?
Screaming from a safe place?
Nine smocked doctors, three unmasked.
One has left his face sewn to the pillow.
One holds a lace fan like a hand of cards she studies,
Considering the risks.

She is the loveliest doctor.
Her doctor-father scolds her right there in front of all the other
    doctors.
They are aghast.
They kneel and don carnival hats with feathers.
I don't think they are really doctors.
The trees are real. They are green Kachinas.
Dark rooms of wind are installed in the house of barbarism.
The norm is always incorrect. If what?

# Rubber Angel

The world is not
Your philosophical problem.

Generous with rigor,
Bright blue regardless of heat,

It flourishes in distance:

The flowers we preserved,
The owl-pocked forests
We defended with spikes.

Just try
Not living your life.
I dare you.

# The Other Reason It Rains, Etc.

*for Ray Worster (1918–1984)*
*and Lyle Van Waning (1922–1988)*

It's going to rain for two reasons.
What do you think the other one is.
Time was there was more room

For things to exist:
Price tags, eyebrows, nuns, dungarees,
surf, weeds, eclipses, radios,

Squirrels, sod, junk, siestas.
Yes there was aspirin. Yes there were cellos.
Yes there was brooding tenderness.

That was when there was haying.
I saw Ray's truck parked next to Lyle's,
Bales in the field, three tractors

And the flatbed idle.
To the east God's anvil about to fall through the floor.
Then I saw those two old friends

Across the creek on the hill
Picking wildflowers.
That was when there were pocket combs and willows,

Rain promise, hay down, time in a stitch.
I picked up bales and drove them to the barn,
Which was like a seed of early night

Inside the late afternoon.

# Small Countries

In defense of whatever happens next, the navy of flat-bottomed popcorn clouds steams over like they are floating down a river we're under. To the west, red cliffs, more pasture, the blue Medicine Bow with stretchmarked snowfields, quartzite faces like sunny bone. I'm worried about Lyle getting back from town with his oxygen, but then I see him through binoculars turn the Studebaker, antlike, off the county road and up the four mile grade, so small down there that I want to imagine his hands on the wheel, still strong, his creased blue jeans and high-top shoes I know he wears to town. He turns off the road on a small knoll about halfway up and stops the truck, facing the mountains. He still looks small against so much space, but I can see his left arm and shoulder and the brim of his hat lowered as he lights a smoke and looks off toward the mountains, and small countries of light and dark rush across the prairie towards him and over him.

# Big Thompson Svaha

Down from the weary, steeply buttressed cirques,
Over snowfat stands of evergreens,
The river gathers rain into her skirts
And hurries it away. Smithereens
Of broken mountains blush and steam and yawn.
There is no word in English for the gap
Between the look of lightning and its clap:
After a moment of deep consideration,

Permission to resume our lives again.
Tomorrow they will pick limp fishermen
From limbs of trees that never meant to bear,
And oldsters from Dubuque will point to where
Their cottage went, while unexploded propane
Tanks bob, nudge, and spin, so unashamed
In the deep, permissionless consideration
That waits for us, birthlight, deathroll, taken.

# Real Wonder

In the stunned little interval
Between winter and spring,
Like the held gasp of surprise
Preceding real wonder,
I'm a flashlight in daylight.

Green stirs low down and shows
Through dead blond shocks of grass,
And gray aspen flowers dangle
Above old snowbanks:
I go around like a feral saint.

The timber hordes
Its meager crust of snow.
I used to walk over the hill
To visit my neighbor
About now.

Just because he was still alive
After another winter.
We'd look out the window
At the groggy meadow,
Not much to say by the end.

This year my neighbor is dead
So I walk the hill anyway.
There's his dead house.
There's his dead fence.
The timber hordes

Its meager crust of snow.
I'm a gunnysack of gravel.
I'm sudden as a gust of light.
This is just

The stunned little interval

After another winter,
The held gasp of surprise
Preceding real wonder.

# Emancipation Denunciation

My favorite word today is *delve*,
Which makes a fair showing
In the upper echelons,
Yet is base in origin, like Abraham Lincoln.
Abraham Lincoln delving the earth
In Illinois.

You can do it to anything.
You can't help it.
Your own pocket.
Always delving into something,
Even if only a little.

But today I'm leaving untouched.
I'm writing to keep from meddling in it.
I'm not going to burden this day
With the sadness of doing,
Of having done, irrevocably.

I'm trying to let those few remaining
Yellow aspen leaves
Hang from their aspen branches forever.
The light is aniline in which
The day, too, hangs
In a pause of wrong weather before winter.

Today I'm not building anything
Out of wood, I'm not tearing down
Motors or visiting neighbors.
I'm not putting in the new
Double-hung window.

All blue and gray and bluish gray,
The prairie unfolded under gunmetal sky,

All the green locked away in the pines.
I'm trying to leave the day untouched,
Smooth as a riverstone, one of many,

The amnesia of its surface, *like glass.*

# Booklearning

There are certain constants
In Shirley's photographs
Of one-room schools in Albany County, Wyoming.

For one thing,
The schoolmarms are the only ones
Whose clothes ever fit.

A few depict the pale ragamuffins
Horseback, sometimes three or four
Astride the one quixotic nag

That brought them.
One shows the four resident scholars
Perched on the roof of their log Alma Mater,

Massive and gloomy as a wooden raft.
But most are more formulaic:
Children mustered against a wall

To stand in gap-toothed rows,
Wildly varying in height and age, pale
In their tight or tentlike collages of clothes,

Their cowboy hats and galoshes,
Fresh as mushrooms from the logdark where they learned.
(Too dim to photograph),

Staring straight into the sun
Of a winter afternoon chosen for its brilliance,
Trying not to blink for long enough.

Indeed these pictures make Albany County
Look much hotter than it is.

The children look like they are burning up

In so much unresisted glare.
Nevermind the snowdrift
Loitering on the right,

Even paler than the squinty grimaces.
When they go back in
They'll all go blind awhile again,

This time in darkness
Where they could see before.
They are learning things

Whose relevance
To the clear light they go home in
Is only promised.

# Western Civilization

*for William Kittredge*

1.

That woman still lives at her ranch.
You can ask her. Maybe
She knows. As near and far

As the rest of us can tell
The barn and sheds were built
In the Great Depression. Someone

Had money and a big idea.
Far and away the biggest
Idea I've ever seen.

Pat says there must've been
A hundred men, shepherds
And shearers, working there.

It's one of those things
That not only is, but seems,
Larger inside than out,

Like a planetarium or an orange,
Even with Wyoming around it,
And real stars flying away.

Just stick your head in there;
Its dark will make you dizzy.
It has an underneath

Too low to stand in unless
You are a sheep. The loft
Vaults like a dusky church.

2.

All that summer
I balanced water,

Coaxing the desert
Into pasture,

With eight cubic feet
Per second for two

Thousand acres.
Horseback, shovel

On my shoulder along
Miles of ditches:

Stalling here,
Releasing there,

Water over
The deepening green,

Keeping it living:
Herons and cranes

Regal in meadows,
Strings of ducklings

Frothing the ditch
To get away.

3.

One day riding ditches I saw Clay.
He was on the hill against the sky,
Flapping his arms at me.
They were going to bulldoze the corrals at the shearing sheds,

Intricate maze of gates and pens
Clay, as a kid, had built with his father,
Before they lost their ranch, before Frank died,
Before the family had to move away.

The new owner was razing everything.
I guess he had some kind of idea.
Clay didn't need any gates, but, as Pat said,
That's Clay.
I met them at the shearing sheds.
Pat held a wrecking bar like a steel snake.
*I just can't stand tearin' apart all them guys's dreams,*
He said, looking shy.
*Hell is when you know where you are.*

4.

On the barn roof a loose piece of tin
Flaps in the wind like a broken wing.
Wyoming whirls in the sun.

Up in the loft a pair of shears,
Oh, fifty or sixty years forgotten there,

Floats in noonlight, bearing up some dust,
Just a pair of spring-steel scissors,
Two knives joined at the hip, with smiling edges.

An owl the color of things left alone
Flaps out of the gable door.

Hell is when you know where you are:
Mazes of pens and gates dreaming sheep;
Miles of ditches dreaming green.

5.

No one living knows
Who built the shearing sheds,

Unless maybe that woman,
And I'm not about to ask her,
Ever since she tried
To stab her husband with a pair of scissors.
He was ninety-one
And barely held her off.
Later she claimed she was just
Trying to cut his heart
Medication out of his shirt
Pocket – dope, she called it –
And the old man had to leave
The ranch, where he didn't last long.

They bulldozed the corrals.
We got forty gates.
We took them someplace safe.

6.

Now the vast, dim barn floats like an ocean liner
Whose doldrums are meadows spinning into brush,
And everywhere you look Wyoming hurries off.

All night the stars make their escape.
In the loft a pair of shears cuts woolly moonlight.
All day a piece of roofing slaps in the wind.

A startled owl flaps out of the gable.
Hell is when you know where you are and it's beautiful.
You saved the gates for nothing.

You balanced the water to keep the green from spinning
Away into sage, the same gray as the wing
That just now shaded your eyes.

# Rintrah Roars

*for John Grant*

My father-in-law writes from Umbria (where peasants eat
songbirds for lunch and pray beneath frescoes by Giotto):
Saturday, 30 Jan. (last day of the season wherein big men can
kill little birds).

Lyndon Johnson, while being escorted by a young Marine
who said, "That one over there is your helicopter, Sir,"
replied, placing his arm around the boy, "Son, they're *all*
my helicopters."

Sam said, "I might be white bread, but there is one pissed-off
nigger in my heart."

McPherson says he doesn't see anything in the world worth
coming back for. He wants to get off the wheel, says, "I don't
want to come back as anything – not even a bumblebee."

So I say, "Oh, Jim, you'd make a good bumblebee," but I was
thinking: That should be enough for anybody's God.

It would be trite to describe the clocksmith's house – the way
it sounded like bees in there. "You can never have enough
clocks in your house." This from a man who had thousands
in his. I asked, "You probably don't even hear them any-
more." He said, "I hear them when they stop."

Lyle said, "It's alright to be a fool; it's just not alright to be
a old fool."

Steve, the banjo wasn't all they smashed. It was every window.
It was every thing I had. You don't want to feel the wind blow
through your house that way.

Another friend said, "I am chained to the earth to pay for the
freedom of my eyes."

# *Agriculture*

*for Richard Borgmann*

Tonight the rain can't stand up straight, but once,
Watching over my shoulder the ten wheeling suns
Of the double siderake rolling newmown hay
Over and over and over and over
Into the windrow like a thick green rope,
I was nothing
But a window sailing through the night,
And once when twenty horses wild together
All winter, galloped towards me down the road
With Harrison whooping behind them and
The little stock dog barking at their heels,
And me there to turn them into the corral
From the middle of the road, their eighty
Hooves a roll of thunder in the earth,
Me with a stupid piece of rope in my hand,
I was nothing
But a window sailing through the night.

# Expecting Company

Death is when the outside world
Wants to get away from itself
By going inside of someone.

Till the walls cave in.
Till the roof is gone.

I'm floating face up
On a sea of adrenaline.
A broken window hangs around my neck.

I have to make more room in here.
I have to get rid of the furniture.

# Winter Road

The reasons the winter road acts so crazy
Are all invisible now.

The summer road persists
In reasoned argument,
Reducing terrain to topography,

Curving gracefully to the left,
Or bending gently to the right,

Gaining, falling, abstracting
Rises, draws, outcrops, woods.

The winter road is crazy.
This time of year it seems
To slam nihilistically

Against the ridgeside,
Sidle through unlikely groves,

Make esses where the summer road goes straight,
Crossing and recrossing,

It dodges to the left, leaps to the right,
A road out of control.

In winter how a road should go
Is told by contours of atmosphere.

The landscape is just a situation
Of windbreaks and wind-permissions.

Heedlessly the summer road
Dives into broad drifts.

It surfaces a couple of times
Between white waves,
Then goes down for good.

Now the winter road is smart to seek
High ground, exposed to wind,

To thread the drifts
Like big white corpses on a field.

Come winter this road proves amazing.
All along it was
In the right place,

Already leaping to the left,
Dodging to the right,

Sailing through contours of atmosphere,
Prophetic and dumb.

# Time Optics

Where the ditch vaults the river,
Where the wooden flume weeps over,
Paying the way,
Where its veil makes a thin distance
And has no critics but wind-in-willowshade,
My love and I lay down
In seventeen kinds of native grasses.
We took our time.
Some wasps were building
A Japanese lantern in the branches,
The flume kept weeping into the river.
Chilly ditchwater.
Don't worry, little wasps, wooden flume,
I'll be alright gone.

# The Sacral Dreams of Ramon Fernandez

*"Ramon Fernandez was not*
*intended to be anyone*
*at all."*
    *– Wallace Stevens*

Ramon Fernandez did not live
As has been suggested,
By the sea.
The unacceptable thoughts
That plagued his dreams
Were diagnosed as being the result
Of unacceptable thoughts.
He could see the stars
Over the San Juan Valley,
Moonlight on the Sangre de Cristo Range.
He could hear,
Despite the constant ringing in his ears,
The feet of *Penitentes*
Scuffling past his low door,
The whistling of their thorn branches.
It all seemed real enough to Ramon,
And not in the least to require his witness.
I'm not saying Ramon Fernandez
Had no imagination.
He could alter the way he saw
Some things, small things,
Like transparent vessels
And birds, both rare and common.
But the mountains were too much for him.
When the *Penitentes* scuffled by moaning,
He hid.

Directly underneath Ramon's fields
An abandoned coal mine smoldered.

It had been abandoned
Because of smoldering.
Every time the wind blew hard
Water in the ditches boiled,
The *acequia* Ramon used
To irrigate his vegetables.
Ramon picked cooked vegetables –
Carrots, turnips, beets –
Out of the steaming soil.
To someone else this might have seemed
Acceptable.
For Ramon it was just the beginning
Of sacral dolor.
For instance,
Ramon Fernandez did not like his father,
Though his father was dying of cancer.
Oh, there were two or three
Paternal qualities
Ramon could list
That might have seemed acceptable
To someone else.
His father was a stoic
To the point of emotionlessness.
His father was a *bultero*.
The *Penitentes* never bothered him!
Then there were Ramon's sisters.
Ramon Fernandez wished
They would leave him alone.
Ramon Fernandez wished they would stop
Praying for him.

His mother had died very young.
Unacceptably young it seemed to Ramon.
It made his ears ring.
He loved his wife and children
With acceptable excess of devotion,
But their mortality –

The idea of it! –
Was unbearable to him.
Furthermore he wanted
To sleep with every woman on earth
Except the ugly ones.
Ramon recognized this feeling
As unacceptable.
When he confessed it to his wife
She made him sleep in the cistern.
Ramon Fernandez it seemed,
Wanted acceptable thoughts
For unacceptable reasons:
To rid himself of chronic lumbar pain,
Gastroenteritis,
Ringing in the ears
And, if possible, to gain
Escape from Hell.

There was, near his house,
On a plateau at the foot
Of the Sangre de Cristo Mountains,
A lake reputed by local myth to be
Unfathomable.
Ramon's solace
Was to lie on the ice at night in winter,
Cruciform, and ponder
The manifest, synchromeshed stars
And the unmanifest
Depths beneath the ice.
He began to think there was only one
Human emotion,
Whose absence was happiness,
Whose anaesthesis was labor,
That loneliness and guilt
Were indistinguishable
Without reference
To the events which triggered them.

The same with love, hate, boredom, nostalgia, envy.

Nostalgia was the worst,
That loneliness for loneliness
That urped over his existence
And immobilized him
With carpal tunnel pain,
Rotator cuff discomfort.
Ramon Fernandez began to think
That all the great philosophers
Were simple fugitives
From the kind of thinking that gives one
Excruciating back pain.
Cowards. Unacceptable.
Especially Neitszche.
Also Heidegger, Freud, Marx.
All cowards. All had cobbled,
From unacceptable thoughts of loneliness,
Escapes that crumpled like paper wings
On the moonlit talus.
Ramon Fernandez was not sure
About mathematicians
Or astronomers.
He could only guess how lonely
Jesus must have been.

Eventually Ramon unstuck himself
And went home to sleep in the cistern,
Which was onion-shaped, chiseled
Out of solid rock,
Inexplicably dry,
With a single, starry opening at the top.
At least Einstein and (Ramon's favorite)
Wallace Stevens had left
A little room for loneliness,
Had heard what it had to say,
Though a great many poets, it seemed,

Had embraced and later died
Of loneliness,
Like a venereal disease.
Having so thought,
Down in the cistern,
Under the terrifying stars,
Ramon turned to the chiseled wall
And away from desire
For acceptability.
There followed,
Without Ramon's volition
Or reference, images
Of eternal principles –
Not ones he would have thought up
By himself.

For example, his burro.
For example the arias of coyotes
Which never frightened his burro.
For example the asters
His burro stepped on
As they rode, in summer, through the San Juan.
Ramon Fernandez considered the *bultos*
And *santos* his father whittled,
The inherent religiosity
Even of secular art.
He considered the *Penitentes*,
The unbelievable spiritual confusion
Of their children.
He considered the missionary aspect of termites.
When he closed his eyes
He could see the mountains perfectly,
But with eyes closed
He could only approximately
Imagine the stars.
His wrists hurt.
He said, *God has brought me here.*

# Woman Walking a One-Kick Dog
# Along an Asymptotic Curve

*for Bert Honea*

Nothing is nothing
Nothing is not nothing
Nothing is next to nothing

## Woman Walking a One-Kick Dog
## Along an Asymptotic Curve II

I am no one.
I am no one else.

# Christmas, 1960

Some of my friends were hoping for BB guns.

I had it over them.

My dad
gave me a .30-.30.

What a great guy.

He gave me ammunition, and when
I fired it, he always stood behind me to catch me when it always knocked
me down.

He was getting me ready to kill a deer that fall.

He taught me
to sit stone-still in a rock outcrop at the bottom of a draw.

He was
going to drive the deer down to me, close enough to kill.

Even a child
could kill that close.

The other thing he taught me was the twenty-
minute nap.

The way you get your sleep in war.

We practiced daily.
Like somebody threw a rock through the window from the outside and
covered the bed with broken glass – that's how I lay next to my father
on the bed while he took his twenty-minute nap, breathing in through
his nose and out through his mouth, and I lay there, light beside him,
under orders.

It wasn't child abuse.

He never touched me.

I would have
levitated if he'd taught me that.

I wasn't napping.

I was not daring
to move for fear he'd wake.

I was paying attention to the aspenwood
paneling, the knots like birds' eyes in the ceiling.

                                        Like Ophelia
was how I felt, as the raptors' eyes grew faces, wings.
                                        My face
felt like it was pushing through from the other side of a looking-glass.

Could I have floated, like the dead, I would.
                                        But like the living, sank.
The birds with eyes, not all of them friendly, swirled over me.
                                        I saw
a drop of blood at the center of everything.
                                        I knew what God was.
                                                          I
knew I was my father's little teddy bear of stone.

# Postcard

Days are cubes of light
That equal each other
Whether anything happens in them or not,
No matter what anyone did or didn't do,
They are equal.

The emptiest are lovely,
Though one is drawn to the bright-edged shards
Of days that cracked
From disappointment and longing.

Some days I go looking for oceans.
If I find one I search the beach
For the teeth I left
In a glass of water
In a motel room in Nebraska.

I'm losing the ability to tremble.
I find appearances helpful.
Some days I go looking for the sky.

NOTE

The last line of "Rintrah Roars" is from Porchia.

Book design and composition by John D. Berry, using Aldus Page-Maker 5.0 and an Apple Macintosh IIvx. The text typeface is Bell Semibold, and the display face is Bell Italic. Bell, which was cut by Richard Austin for John Bell's type foundry in 1788, is considered to be the first English modern type. Bell was revived for hot-metal type-setting by the English Monotype company in 1932, and was later expanded into a three-weight digital type family, again by Monotype. Printed by Thomson-Shore, Inc.

The new Copper Canyon Press logo is the Chinese character for poetry, and is pronounced *shi*. It is composed of two simple characters: the righthand character is the phonetic and means "temple" or "hall," while the lefthand character means "speech" or "word." The calligraphy is by Yim Tse, who teaches at the University of British Columbia.